Charles Sullivan

ALPHABET
ANIMALS

RIZZOLI
NEW YORK

Muddy Alligators by John Singer Sargent, 1917

A is for ALLIGATOR

Alligators live

in muddy old swamps;

the noises they make

are *splashes* and *chomps*.

John Singer Sargent (1856-1925). American artist famous for his superb portraits of men and women; he also produced lively watercolors and oil paintings of distant places.

B is for BEAR

The bear is as big

as a house,

but the friend she likes best

is a mouse.

George Catlin (1796-1872). American artist best known for his colorful and striking paintings of Indians and the Old West.

Portraits of Grizzly Bear and Mouse, from Life, by George Catlin, 1832

5

Amelia C. Van Buren and Cat by Thomas Eakins, about 1891

C is for CAT

This cat

would rather look at you

than at a picture book.

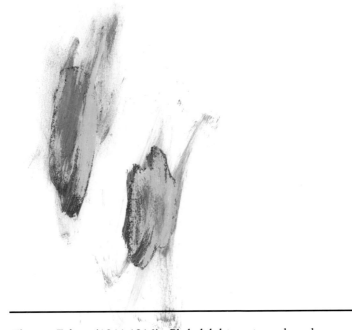

Thomas Eakins (1844-1916). Philadelphia artist and teacher, one of
the great American portraitists; the young woman in his photograph
is Amelia Van Buren, a student.

D is for DINOSAUR

If I could find a dinosaur

I know just how I'd ride him–

I'd make believe he was my car

but never get inside him.

Jim Gary (1939-). Working in New Jersey, he puts together large
"dinosaurs" out of old automobile parts. His creations are especially popular
with children, and he encourages their creativity, too.

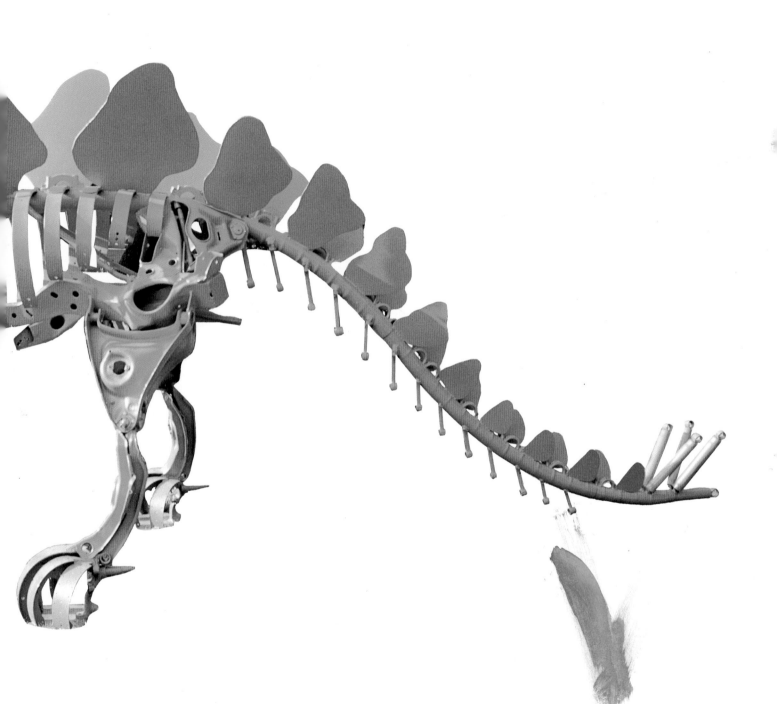

Stegosaurus by Jim Gary, 1987

Elephant by Rembrandt, 1637

E is for ELEPHANT

Elephants have noses

like hoses;

when they play

they spray

almost everyone–

and think it's fun.

Rembrandt (van Rijn) (1606-1669). A productive and influential Dutch artist whose paintings, prints, and drawings embrace classical subjects as well as everyday scenes.

F is for FOX

"Let's go for a walk in the snow,"

said the fox;

"I'll fly through the sky

with my friends,"

said the crow.

Winslow Homer (1836-1910). An American magazine illustrator and powerful, original artist, his subjects include the Civil War, the Maine seacoast, and vivid outdoor scenes with children.

The Fox Hunt by Winslow Homer, 1893

Giraffe by anonymous painter, 19th century

G is for GIRAFFE

Half a giraffe

is a neck so long

it takes hours to laugh

or to sing a song.

H is for HARE

A rabbit looks like a hare,

a hare looks like a rabbit–

isn't that funny?

But I don't care,

for I'm in the habit

of calling all of them "bunny."

Albrecht Dürer (1471-1528). German painter and printmaker, who is considered the greatest artist of the Northern European Renaissance.

The Hare by Albrecht Dürer, 1502

Head of a Horned Animal, Iranian sculpture, 6-5th century B.C.

I is for IBEX

This is the head of an ibex:

a mountain-climbing goat

that leaps so high

in the dreamy sky

it almost seems to float.

J is for JAGUAR

Can you hang from a tree

like me?

And when you've hung

for a while,

can you stick out your tongue

and smile?

Loren McIntyre (1917-). American writer-photographer, based in Virginia, who travels the world in search of interesting subjects.

Jaguar Lazing in Tree by Loren McIntyre

K is for KANGAROO

If you were a kangaroo,

and your mother was, too,

would you travel in her pouch–

BUMP/BOUNCE, BUMP/BOUNCE, BUMP/BOUNCE–

and never once say "*ouch*"?

Alexander Calder (1898-1976). American artist whose works range from delicate jewelry and small animal sculptures to huge abstract mobiles (hanging objects) and stabiles (standing objects).

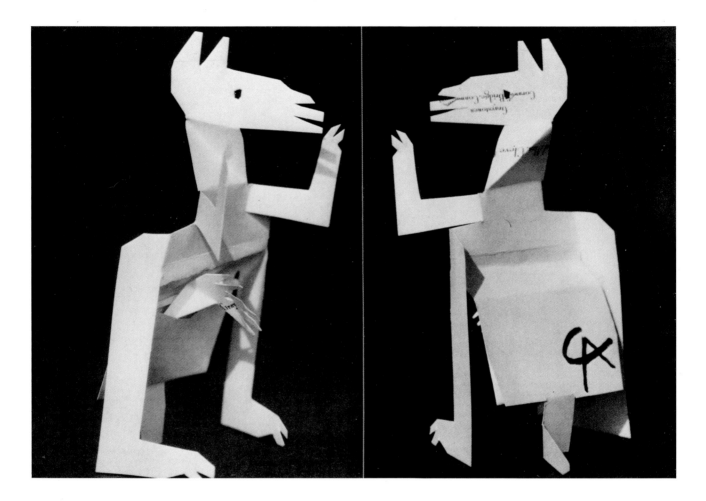

Birth-Announcement Kangaroo by Alexander Calder, 1959

Lioness and Cub in East Africa's Serengeti by Mitsuaki Iwago

L is for LION

As still as statues

in the shade of a hill,

these lions see something;

soon they will roar

and start to explore.

Mitsuaki Iwago. Japanese photographer whose work appears in *National Geographic* and many other publications.

Tropical Forest with Monkeys by Henri Rousseau, 1910

M is for MONKEY

Monkeys in the tropics

discuss the latest topics,

but some of them spend hours

just smelling the flowers.

Henri Rousseau (1844-1910). French primitive painter best known for his dreamlike pictures of animals in jungles and other exotic settings.

N is for NANNY GOAT

Goats may look the same

though they have different names:

"billy" is a father goat,

"nanny" is a mother,

sister goat is called a "kid,"

brother is another.

Marc Chagall (1887-1985). Early modern artist, born in Russia, who settled in France but recaptured the village scenes of his childhood in fanciful paintings, stained glass, mosaics, and lithographs.

Maternity by Marc Chagall, 1925

Ox-Driver by Ishikawa Toyonobu, 18th century

O is for OX

The hungry ox

goes slowly past

this basket full

of tasty grass.

Ishikawa Toyonobu (1711-1785). Best known as a printmaker, this Japanese artist was able to present his scenes of everyday life with elegance, energy, and great skill.

Porcupine by
Leonard Baskin,
1951

P is for PORCUPINE

A porcupine was a friend of mine

but I couldn't give her a hug,

and she kept getting caught in the rug,

so I sent her a valentine.

Leonard Baskin (1922-). American artist whose strong sense of design includes calligraphy and illustration as well as sculpture, painting, and printmaking.

 **is for QUARTER HORSE**

The quarter horse

goes very fast,

a quarter of a mile;

the cowboy knows

its speed won't last

more than a little while.

Frederic Remington (1861-1909). The cowboy's life in the Old West is very real and dramatic in the paintings of this hard-riding American artist.

The Cowboy by Frederic Remington, 1902

Black Rhinoceros by Andy Warhol, 1983

R is for RHINOCEROS

If a cross

rhinoceros

decides to follow me,

I think I'll follow him

instead, or climb

the nearest tree.

Andy Warhol (1928-1987). Controversial American Pop artist and filmmaker who sometimes used bold and disturbing color combinations to achieve startling effects.

S is for SQUIRREL

When the cold wind scatters

nuts among the leaves,

this old squirrel chatters

as though he believes

that nothing else matters.

John James Audubon (1785-1851). American painter who combined
a passionate love of nature with scientific accuracy and detail; his *Birds
of America* appeared in four illustrated volumes (1827-1838).

Soft-Haired Squirrel by John James Audubon, about 1845

T is for TIGER

Playing with his mother,

the young tiger must be careful;

there are claws in his paws

and in hers.

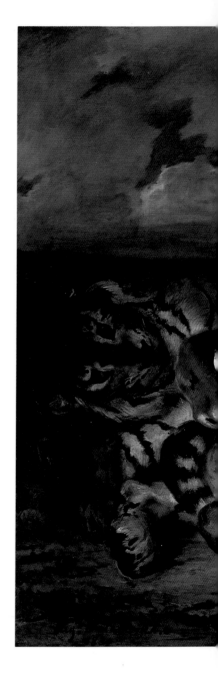

Eugène Delacroix (1798-1863). A prolific French painter
of the Romantic period, whose animals, people, and other
subjects are depicted with great vigor and imagination.

40

Young Tiger Playing with His Mother by Eugène Delacroix, 1830

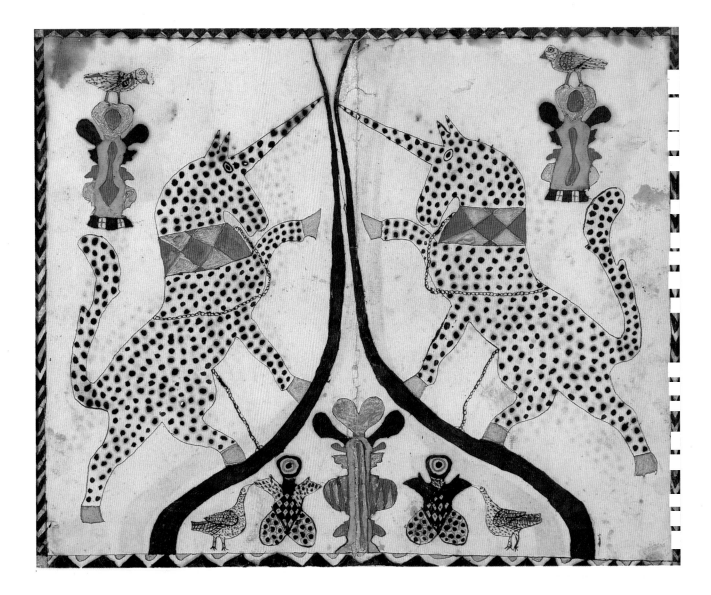

Unicorns (Fraktur), about 1795-1830

U is for UNICORN

Unicorns

have single horns

and wish that they had many,

but they are not real animals–

they really haven't any.

V is for VETERINARIAN

Here is a sick pet–

a possum that swallowed a bug–

and this doctor is the "vet"

who will make him well and snug.

Brad Graverson (1954-). California photographer whose candid
pictures of American life appear in newspapers, books, and magazines.

Dr. Alice Villalobos, Veterinarian, by Brad Graverson, 1984

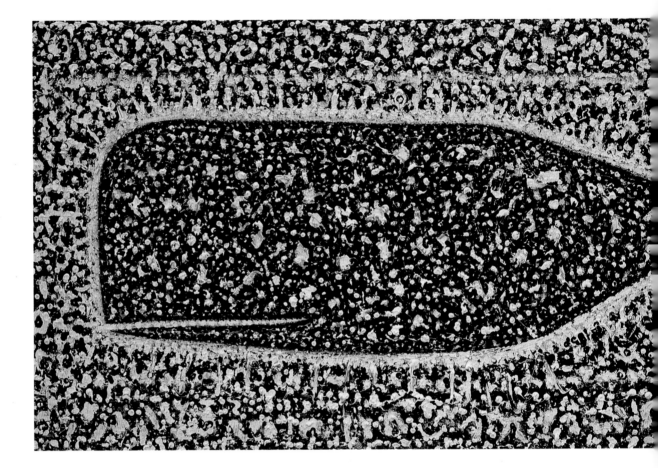

Save the Whale by Richard Pousette-Dart, 1980

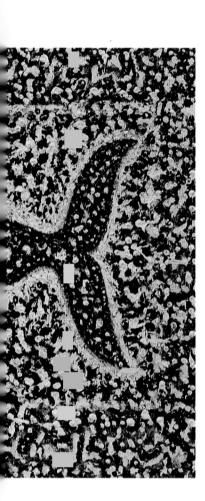

W is for WHALE

I wish I could swim

like a fish,

or make a big SPLASH

with my tail,

like a whale.

Richard Pousette-Dart (1916-). American "abstract
expressionist" artist whose recent work has used basic
shapes and colors to convey the mysteries of the universe.

Rex #2 by Alex Katz, 1975

X is for REX

D is for Dog, I agree,

but Rex is *my* dog–so he

must have a special place

to show his hairy face.

Alex Katz (1927-). Considered one of the best modern portraitists, this American artist often presents a simplified view of the head and shoulders of his subjects, human or animal, in order to reveal their character.

Study for *The Unruly Calf* by Winslow Homer, about 1875

Y is for YEARLING

A yearling is an animal

whose age is one,

not two—

how old are you?

Winslow Homer (1836-1910). An American magazine illustrator and powerful, original artist, his subjects include the Civil War, the Maine seacoast, and vivid outdoor scenes with children.

Zebra by Henry Moore, 1979

Z is for ZEBRA

Zebras are white

with black stripes,

or maybe they are black

with white–

I'm not sure which

is right.

Henry Moore (1898-1986). British artist best known for large abstract sculptures of people, but he also portrayed animals realistically.

AUTHOR'S NOTE

Learning the alphabet was one of the greatest thrills of my childhood–I can still remember the pride and satisfaction I felt when I could finally say it without a mistake: "A, B, C" right through to "X, Y, Z." Where was the hardest part? Somewhere around the middle, I think: "J, K, L, M, N."

In those days, the letters of the alphabet were considered as building-blocks to learning words: once I knew "C, A, T" I could soon spell "CAT" (and later "ACT"). But the letters themselves were meaningless at first, connected only to the ones before and after them when the correct order was memorized.

Today a child can learn the alphabet more quickly and easily by associating the various letters with meaningful words (or pictures) from the beginning. "A is for Apple, B is for Ball," and so on.

In this book, I have chosen to associate each letter with the name of an animal (alligator, bear, cat, etc.) or something else in the world of animals (unicorn, veterinarian). Each animal is represented visually by a work of art or by an exceptionally fine photograph. For example, the alligators appear in a watercolor by John Singer Sargent, the bear in an oil painting by George Catlin, and the cat in a photograph by Thomas Eakins. This, I believe, is the first time that really significant works of art have been used in a book intended primarily for young children.

Each animal is also represented by a poem I have written. The poetry is deliberately varied in terms of mood, rhythm, rhyme, and sentence structure, so that young readers can begin to enjoy the different shadings and tones of poems, just as they learn to enjoy the differences among pictures. I am eager to hear from readers of all ages–do you like this book, what do you like best, is there anything about it that you don't like? Please write and tell me what you think (my address is: Post Office Box 1775, Annapolis, MD 21404). I am especially looking forward to the reactions of two young readers who happen to be my grandchildren: Edward Louis Sullivan, born in February, 1991, and Frank Hannafee Sullivan, just two years old at that time. Let me hear from you.

One thing more–a special note of thanks to Lois Brown, my editor.

CHARLES SULLIVAN
WASHINGTON, D.C.

ACKNOWLEDGMENTS

Anonymous. *Giraffe*, American 19th century. Stencil and watercolor, 12 1/8 x 12 1/2". M. and M. Karolik Collection. Courtesy, Museum of Fine Arts, Boston.

John James Audubon. *Soft-Haired Squirrel*, about 1845. Watercolor on paper, 11 1/4 x 16". Wadsworth Atheneum, Hartford. Gift of Henry Schnakenberg.

Leonard Baskin. *Porcupine*, 1951. Woodcut, 21 x 29". Print Collection, Miriam & Ira D. Wallach Division of Art, Prints and Photographs. The New York Public Library. Astor, Lenox and Tilden Foundations.

Alexander Calder. Line drawings from *Animal Sketching*, reproduced with kind permission of David A. Boehm, Publisher and Chairman, Sterling Publishing Corporation, Inc.

Alexander Calder. *Birth-Announcement Kangaroo*, 1959. Paper, height 6". Mr. and Mrs. Cleve Gray, Cornwall Bridge, Connecticut.

George Catlin. *Portraits of Grizzly Bear and Mouse, from Life*, 1832. Oil on canvas, 26 1/2 x 32 1/2". © National Museum of American Art, Smithsonian Institution, Gift of Mrs. Joseph Harrison, Jr. 1985.66.603.

Marc Chagall. *Maternity*, 1925. Photo Philippe Migeat. Copyright © Centre Georges. Pompidou, Musée National d'Art Moderne, Paris.

Eugène Delacroix. *Young Tiger Playing with His Mother*, 1830. Canvas, 1,30 x 1,95 m. Musée du Louvre, Paris.

Albrecht Dürer. *Der Hase* (The Hare), 1502. Watercolor and gouache. Graphische Sammlung Albertina, Vienna.

Thomas Eakins. *Amelia C. Van Buren and Cat*, about 1891. Platinum Print, 6 3/4 x 8". David Hunter McAlpin Fund, 1943. The Metropolitan Museum of Art, New York.

Fraktur, (Unicorn), c. 1795-1830. Ink and watercolor. Courtesy, Henry Francis du Pont Winterthur Museum. 61.1113

Jim Gary. *Stegosaurus*, 1987. Metal sculpture made from discarded automobile parts. Courtesy the artist and Longwood Gardens.

Brad Graverson. *Dr. Alice Villalobos, Veterinarian*. Photograph black-and-white. Copyright © 1984 by Brad Graverson. Courtesy the artist and NewSage Press.

Winslow Homer. *The Fox Hunt*, 1893. Oil on canvas, 38 x 68 1/2". Courtesy of the Pennsylvania Academy of the Fine Arts, Philadelphia, Joseph E. Temple Fund. 1894.4.

Winslow Homer. Study for *The Unruly Calf*, about 1875. Pencil with chinese white on paper, 4 3/4 x 8 1/2". The Brooklyn Museum. 28.241, Museum Collection Fund.

Mitsuaki Iwago. Lioness and Cub in East Africa's Serengeti. Photograph. Copyright © 1989 Mitsuaki Iwago.

Iranian, Achaemenid. *Head of a Horned Animal*, 6-5th century B.C. Metalwork-bronze, h. 13 3/8" Copyright © 1990, The Metropolitan Museum of Art, Fletcher Fund, 1956. (56.45).

Alex Katz. *Rex #2*, 1975. Oil on canvas, 78 x 90". Private Collection, Courtesy Marlborough Gallery, New York.

Loren McIntyre. Jaguar Lazing in Tree. Photograph. Courtesy Loren McIntyre.

Henry Moore. *Zebra*, 1979. Carbon line, crayon, conte crayon. Copyright © Henry Moore Foundation 1979, #79 (149). By kind permission of the Henry Moore Foundation.

Richard Pousette-Dart. *Save the Whale*, 1980. Acrylic on canvas, 1.1 x 2.1 m. Courtesy the artist.

Rembrandt (van Rijn). *Ein Elefant* (An Elephant), 1637. Black chalk. Graphische Sammlung Albertina, Vienna.

Frederic Remington. *The Cowboy*, 1902. Oil on canvas. Amon Carter Museum, Forth Worth, Texas.

Henri Rousseau. *Tropical Forest with Monkeys*, 1910. Oil on canvas, 51 x 64". National Gallery of Art, Washington. John Hay Whitney Collection. 1982.76.7 (2873).

John Singer Sargent. *Muddy Alligators*, 1917. Watercolor over graphite on off-white wove paper. Worcester Art Museum, Worcester, Massachusetts. 1917.86.

Ishikawa Toyonobu. *Mitate* (Ox-Driver), 18th century, Edo Period. O-ban Benizuri-e, Tokyo National Museum, Tokyo.

Andy Warhol. *Black Rhinoceros*, 1983 from *Endangered Species* series. Screenprint on Lenox Museum board, 38 x 38". Copyright © 1990 The Estate and Foundation of Andy Warhol/ARS NY.

title page illustration:
Alexander Calder. Line drawings from *Animal Sketching*, reproduced with
kind permission of David A. Boehm, Publisher and Chairman, Sterling
Publishing Co., Inc.

First published in the United States of America in 1991 by
Rizzoli International Publications, Inc.
300 Park Avenue South, New York, New York 10010

Library of Congress Cataloging-in-Publication Data

Sullivan, Charles, 1933-
    Alphabet Animals

Summary: An ABC illustrated with paintings, sculpture, and photographs of
animals from American and international museum collections.
    1. Animals–Pictorial works–Juvenile literature.
2. English language–Alphabet–Juvenile literature.
3. Animals in art–Juvenile literature. 4. Alphabet. 5. Animals in art. I. Title.
Ql49.S83 1991 [E] 90-28316
ISBN 0-8478-1377-0

Design by Nai Y. Chang

Printed and bound in Singapore